D1187903

This copy of

A Mother's
Treasury of Prayer

comes to

....

with love from

....

Copyright © 1996 Eagle. Compiled by Sue Wavre.
For a list of the sources of quotations in this book, please see page 88.
All unattributed prayers written by Sue Wavre.

British Library Cataloguing-in-Publication Data. A catalogue record
for this book is available from the British Library.

Published in the UK by Eagle, an imprint of Inter Publishing Service
(IPS) Ltd, St Nicholas House, 14 The Mount, Guildford, Surrey GU2
5HN.

Printed in Singapore

ISBN: 0 86347 166 8

A

Mother's

Treasury of Prayer

eagle

Guildford, Surrey

Illustrations

The illustrations in this book were all painted by Helen Allingham, between 1882 and 1904. All are reproduced © IPS Ltd.

Contents

Mother's Spirituality

There is nothing more important than our relationship with God. In all the hectic whirl of life – when there seems to be no time for him – we need him. There are periods when it is almost impossible to be quiet, but he is always there beside us. Talk to him, listen to him, read a verse or two of a psalm if you have no time for more of his Word, but don't leave him out of your motherhood.

Be still, and know that I am God.
Psalm 46:10

Surrender in prayer

Lord, I surrender myself to let the Holy Spirit pray through me for the needs of my friends and family members. Show me the things that are on your heart so I may pray more effectively. Help me to be more diligent to pray in the Spirit as you direct, knowing that I am praying according to your will. I thank you for the precious gift of the Holy Spirit. In Jesus' name, Amen.

Quin Sherrer

Time with God

Time for myself. ... Why is it that I find it so hard to take time for myself? Time to be rather than to do. Time to think, to talk to God, and most of all to be silent in his presence while he talks to me.

You know how it is, Lord! There is always so much to be fitted in. People to be seen ... obligations to fulfil! It is so difficult to distinguish between the urgent and the important. And often what is urgent elbows its way to the forefront of my day and the important gets trampled on in the rush.

Slow me down, Lord. Teach me the art of creating islands of stillness, in which I can absorb the beauty of everyday things: clouds, trees, a snatch of music. Prompt me to lift up my heart to you in a moment of thankfulness. Impress upon my mind that there is more to life than packing every moment with activity, and help me to fence in some part of my day with quietness.

And please talk to me and help me to listen, so that I take your peace rather than my confusion back with me into the hurly-burly of a hurting world.

Marion Stroud

Sitting quietly

Lord, if only I had more time.
Time for you.
Time to think and relax; to get to know you better.
Time to develop that relationship I need so much.
But I have time!
I'm sitting here now, writing, reading.
Maybe not for long, but it is time.
How shall I use it, Lord? ...
Maybe I'll just sit quietly with you.
Letting in your healing.
Thank you.

Eddie Askew

I surrender my activity to you

Lord, the next time I find myself thinking, "I'm only playing with the children," or "I'm only sorting the washing," help me to stop saying "only". Even when I'm tired, help me to surrender my activity to you, so that I can give myself fully to what needs doing. Let me remember that this is your will for me, here and now, and show me how to receive the good things and the gladness that you offer me.

Angela Ashwin

Just for today

Oh, God, give me grace for this day. Not for a lifetime, nor for next week, nor for tomorrow, just for this day.
Direct my thoughts and bless them.
Direct my work and bless it.
Direct the things I say, and give them blessing too.
Direct and bless everything that I think and speak and do. So that for this one day, just this one day, I have the gift of grace that comes from your presence.
Oh God, for this day, just this one day, let me live generously, kindly, in a state of grace and goodness that denies my many imperfections and makes me more like you.

Marjorie Holmes

When I can't pray

And when the times come when we can't pray, it is very simple: if Jesus is in my heart let Him pray, let me allow Him to pray in me, to talk to His Father in the silence of my heart. Since I cannot speak – He will pray.

Mother Theresa

Birth and Babies

Can a mother forget the baby at her breast
and have no compassion on the child
she has borne?
Though she may forget,
I will not forget you!
Isaiah 49:15

Jesus said,
'Let the little children come to me,
and do not hinder them,
for the kingdom of heaven
belongs to such as these.'
Matthew 19:14

Awaiting the birth

A baby is on the way, Lord, and our hearts are filled with ever-increasing delight as we marvel at the awesome mystery of being co-creators with you. Even while we parents-to-be rejoice in being recipients of your love and the instruments of your will, we regard with apprehension this responsibility that is ours. We feel so much the need of relating more deeply to you. We look forward with expectancy and joy to the birth of our child. As we cling more closely to one another, we commit ourselves to you, resting in the confidence that this baby is in your embrace, that you will care for our child and us. We pray that each of us and our child may be your children and your beloved servants forever.

Leslie and Edith Brandt

Alleluia

Alleluia, Alleluia, Alleluia, O, my God, My soul rejoices in God." I never thought I could love a tiny creature so much. Bless my baby now and forever. Make me a good mother. Lord Jesus watch over us.

Ronda De Sola Chervin

Thanksgiving

O God, our Father, we give you thanks for this little child who has come to us from you. Bless her now and all the days of her life. Protect her in the days of her helplessness; bring her in safety through childhood's dangers; and grant that she may grow to adulthood and do a good day's work and witness for you. Help us her parents so to love her and so to train her that we will not fail in the trust which you have given to us, and that, even as you have given her to us, we may give her back in dedication to you: through Jesus Christ our Lord. Amen.

William Barclay

I'm tired

O Lord, help me. I am so tired, so tired. I love this little child, but I am physically and emotionally worn out. Infants are demanding – late nights, daybreak mornings, unpredictable schedules. I keep waiting for things to get back to normal, only to realise that this is now normal. And I never dreamed how emotionally unstrung I would feel. I don't understand why the baby is crying. The baby doesn't respond to me as a person. I'm depressed. I feel alone. Calm me, Lord. This will end soon. Schedules will emerge. Baby will sleep longer. I will be more energetic. I can find satisfactions if not in meaningful coos and smiles then in the warmth of a baby close to me, needing me. I can ... share my feelings with my husband, call friends who are glad to listen or talk awhile, call the doctor to ask all my 'little' questions, ... and I can snatch every spare moment of rest possible. Help me relax as I realize an infant is more than smiles, rosy cheeks, and affectionate sounds. But a child, a new baby, is a miracle – new, ongoing life in your creation. Thank you.

Judith Mattison (adapted)

Mothers of Young Children

Train a child in the way he should go,
and when he is old he will not turn from it.
Proverbs 22:6

Take time to be tender.
Fragile and delicate are the feelings
of [our children].
They need to sense we are there
because we care, not just
because it's our job.
Charles Swindoll

Help in teaching virtues

Lord, help me to know how to encourage my children to be kind, patient, generous, pure-minded and self-controlled. Father help me to be able to teach these by example, to develop these same virtues in my own life.

What my child needs

Father, help me to remember and help me to put into practice these wise words:

If a child lives with criticism
    He learns to condemn.
If a child lives with hostility
    He learns to fight.
If a child lives with ridicule
    He learns to be shy.
If a child lives with shame
    He learns to feel guilty.
If a child lives with tolerance
    He learns to be patient.
If a child lives with encouragement
    He learns confidence.
If a child lives with praise
    He learns to appreciate.
If a child lives with fairness
    He learns justice.
If a child lives with security
    He learns to have faith.
If a child lives with approval
    He learns to like himself.
If a child lives with acceptance and friendship
    He learns to find love in the world.

Dorothy Law Nolte

Starting school

O God, our Father, our child is going to school for the first time today; and we cannot help being anxious at this first step away from home.

Keep (name) safe from all that would hurt him(her) in body or harm him(her) in mind.

Help him(her) to be happy at school and to know the joy of learning and playing together with other boys and girls.

Help him(her) to learn well that he(she) may grow up to stand on his(her) own feet, to earn his(her) own living, and to serve you and his (her) fellow men; through Jesus Christ our Lord, Amen.

William Barclay

To love God's Word

O God, help me to influence my child with a love for Your holy Word. Let the Scripture come alive. Let it be more than stories and legend. Let it be Your living breath, Your very voice to my child. Give my child the capacity to hide Your Word in his or her heart so that when difficult circumstances occur, my child will be able to find Your Word.

William and Nancie Carmichael

Taking time

They are only little once, Lord.
Grant me the wisdom and patience
to teach them to follow in your footsteps
and prepare them for what is to come.
They are only little once, Lord.
Make me take the time to play pretend,
to read or tell a story; to cuddle.
Don't let me for one minute
think anything is more important
than the school play,
the recital, the big game, fishing,
or the quiet walk hand in hand.
All too soon, Lord,
they will grow away
and there is no turning back.
Let me have my memories with no regrets.
Please help me to be a good parent, Lord.
When I must discipline,
let me do it in love,
let me be firm, but fair;
let me correct and explain with patience.
They are growing away, Lord.
While I have the chance
let me do my best for them.
For the rest of our lives, please, Lord,
let me be their very best friend.

Mary L. Robbins

What's right for my children?

Father, I just don't know what is best for my children. There are so many things I am anxious about, such as what out of school activities they should take part in.

So many sports clubs meet and play on Sundays now, does that mean my children can't be in the team?

Then at home there's TV.

How much should I allow them to watch?

None at all, or should I just be much stricter on what they can and cannot watch?

I confess I often use that time to do other things; should I watch with them so I know what they are soaking up, so we can talk about it and so I can therefore be more careful about what I let them watch?

Please, Lord, show me what is best and help me to make wise decisions.

Thank you, Lord

For all these smallnesses I thank You, Lord:
    small children and small needs;
    small meals to cook, small talk to heed,
and a small book from which to read
small stories; small hurts to heal
small disappointments, too, as real as ours;
small glories to discover in bugs, pebbles,
flowers.

When day is through my mind is small, my
    strength is gone;
    and as I gather each dear one
I pray, "Bless each for Jesus' sake –
such angels sleeping, imps awake!"

What wears me out are little things:
    angels minus shining wings.
    Forgive me, Lord, if I have whined;
    it takes so much to keep them shined;
    yet each small rub has its reward,
    for they have blessed me.
        Thank you, Lord.

Ruth Bell Graham

Each one is special

Father, thank you for my children – each one unique and special. Help me not to compare them to each other but rather allow them to develop in the way you intend for them, and to love and encourage them.

May I never make one feel inferior to the other or less loved, just because they are gifted in different areas.

I need God's help

Lord, sometimes I am frightened by the weight I feel to bring up these children that you have entrusted to me because in our time, full of confusion and potential, it seems harder and harder to know how to raise children.

I know that I will make mistakes, that I will fail my children, that my strength and patience will not be sufficient, that I will make the wrong decisions, and that at times my love will grow weak.

Around me I see parents labouring under the same weight, afraid in the same way, trying their best, reading, feeling, growing to stay close to their children so that they will have the best possible start.

Help us all to keep love going, and put your blessing on our love which then has a chance to overcome all the mistakes we will make. Help us to know what it means practically to be real companions to our children.

Ulrich Schaffer

Friends for my child

Lord, I am so grateful for my children's friends.
Thank you for each one of them.
I pray that I may never allow my children
    to play with children who would be bad
    for them.
Just because they might be attractive or wealthy
    or intelligent
When they lack the goodness that means so
    much more.
Please send the friends to my children you
    want for them.

Ronda De Sola Chervin

For learning and wisdom

Lord, may my child like Daniel show "... aptitude for every kind of learning, [be] well informed, quick to understand and qualified to serve ..." (Daniel 1:4). May he speak with "wisdom and tact, and may he be found to have a keen mind and knowledge and understanding and also the ability ... to solve difficult problems" (Daniel 2:14; 5:12). Lord, endow my child with "wisdom and ... understanding as measureless as the sand on the seashore" (1 Kings 4:29).

Quin Sherrer (adapted)

Teenagers

To love appropriately sometimes demands difficult decisions. It sometimes requires unpopular restrictions. Unless you are secure in yourself and in the Lord, you will find yourself torn in shreds emotionally, an insecurity that will express itself in the nagging syndrome teenagers so dread.

Joyce Huggett

Anger at my teenager

My God, I try to be patient with my teenage children, but then when they defy me openly I burst into anger and sarcasm.

I realize that only divine grace can bring patient and firm loving kindness free from uncontrolled anger.

I ask you, Holy Spirit, to direct me to the counsel I need from friends or professionals so that I may learn how to deal with teen disobedience in the right way.

Ronda De Sola Chervin

Help me to trust for my child

O God, you know how worried and anxious I am about (name). Help me to be sensible and to see that worrying about things does not make them any better.

Help me to be trustful, and to do all that I can, and then to leave the rest to you

William Barclay

I release my children to you

I release my children to you, Lord. You know the temptations, the dangers they are up against: drugs, sex, the lie that girls must be skinny to be attractive, dangerous driving, drinking – the list is endless.

I ask you to send angels to watch over them and protect them in all their ways. Amen.

The storms of life

I pray that my children will know the peace that passes understanding in the midst of life with all its storms.

I pray that they will know immediately the Prince of Peace, Jesus, who is able to keep them sheltered, covered by His peace as they keep their minds focused on Him.

William and Nancie Carmichael

To encourage them in your ways

Save me, Lord, from the temptation of wanting my children to suceed just for worldly glory or my own pride. May they never believe that I think success in grades is more important than growth in wisdom. Yet I believe that I should pray that they do well if in this way they will have more chance later to serve you as a Christian in the world. Please give me wisdom so that I can encourage my children in the directions that are truly your will.

Grace Geist (adapted)

Forgive my children

Father, I pray for my teenage children, they pretend to be so tough, but you and I know how weak and floundering they are.

I beg you to give them the grace to realize that what attracts them so much in sin is not the pleasure but the fantasy of the pleasure.

Send the Holy Spirit to show them that sin tastes stale the next day so that they will not listen to the lies of the Evil One.

And if they fail and fall, please bring them back swiftly to the haven of your forgiving love.

Helen Ross

Learning the joy of giving

Lord, help my child to be a giver rather than a taker. Help my child to experience the joy of giving. May my child be swift to give time, talent, money, possessions, thanks, compliments, healing words, smiles, love, hugs, and a hand or an ear, whenever the opportunity presents itself.

William and Nancie Carmichael

My teenage daughter

Dear God,
thank you for my lovely daughter.
Thank you for the fun we have together.

Lord, as she grows up so quickly and goes through these teenage years, please protect her, and may her good qualities sustain her and enable her to be strong in the many temptations she will meet.

Help me to trust you that she is safe in your hands, and please give me wisdom and understanding so that I may know how to guide her through this time.

Help me as I struggle

Lord, please, I need guidance in dealing with my rebellious child. Whatever I say seems to make things worse. Give me hope, patience both with my child but also with myself as I struggle, and trust, as I come to you at the end of my tether.

Affirming my child

Lord, sometimes I feel so bad at how harsh I am with my child, how judgmental – wanting him(her) to be perfect! Forgive me and help me to see and focus on the good and lovely qualities in him(her). Instead of criticizing or comparing with others, show me how to affirm my child and to show the depth of my love and acceptance.

Ronda De Sola Chervin (adapted)

I'm afraid for my child

O Jesus, you see into the heart of this mother, so stricken with sorrow and wrenched with fear about her teenage child whose path has so much deviated from yours. You know how much I want to see my child back on the right road, your road.

I renounce my passionate desire to see the conversion of my child right away, and ask instead only to be given a complete trust in the final salvation of (name), my child, and your beloved.

Ronda De Sola Chervin

For right goals

Heavenly Father, please give our children the right goals. Keep them from drifting, from going with the crowd to gain popularity and plenty of friends. Please enable them to sort out their strengths and weaknesses. Help them to see their talents and abilities, not as accidents of birth or a random combination of genes, but as gifts from yourself, to be treasured, developed and used in living life as you, God, mean it to be lived. And help them to have their priorities right. Then the rest of life's concerns will fall into place.

So we would ask you Father – please give our children the right goals.

Marion Stroud

For safe driving

O Jesus! You know how inexperienced a driver my child is in spite of passing his(her) driving test! And you know what's out there: drunken drivers, drivers who are just plain dangerous – other youngsters showing off. Please help my child to drive safely and protect him(her). Here's another time I must learn to hand over my child and trust you, Lord.

Adult children

When I was a child, I talked like a child,
I thought like a child,
I reasoned like a child.
When I became [an adult]
I put childish ways behind me.
1 Corinthians 13:11

To let go of them

Teach me how to let go of my young adult children trusting that my surrender will be for their good and that complete communion will be in heaven.

Ronda De Sola Chervin

A blessing

I pray they will find godly husbands/wives and together they will love the Lord their God with all their hearts, all their souls, with all their strength, and with all their minds, and love their neighbours as themselves (Luke 10:27).

Quin Sherrer

She's leaving home

Dearest Jesus, You gave me a mother's heart and now I feel as if it is breaking. My lovely twenty-year-old daughter is ready to move out of our house. I am tightly holding on to her to keep her within heart's reach at least.

I should be pleased that she is preparing to be an adult now. Why has this left me feeling like a lonely, sad child?

Please give me the gift of courage to release her to your plans for her life.

No matter how much I love her, you, Jesus, love her so much more than I am able to.

You see down the road all that her life holds for her and I am only blinded by my tears and fears.

I ask for the gift to trust you. She was a gift from you. Help me to give her back to you.

Elaine Seonbuchner

Restore my son

Oh, God, please help my son. He has no direction, no goal. He's wandered away from so much that he used to be, or that you, his creator, would have him be.

And I'm not only worried sick about this, God, I feel guilty. I search my own behaviour asking, "Why? Why? What have I done to bring this about? Where have we, his family, failed?"

Dear God, please find and restore him. Arouse in him a sense of purpose, steady him, set him upon his rightful path, and walk with him. We who love him can't do it. Only you who love him even more can do it.

I offer him to you now, whole and beautiful and filled with promise, the way you sent him to us. Thank you for helping him become the person you meant him to be.

Marjorie Holmes

To keep their vows

I pray that my childen will have the courage to give themselves to God and know that He is the love that will never let them go. And in the security of that love, may my children learn to keep their life promises, the vows and the covenants that shape their lives.

William and Nancie Carmichael

Disappointment in my child

Jesus, I wanted so much to see my child flourishing with the talents I know are there.
Today I have to realize that he(she) is not travelling on the path I chose.
Help me to believe that you will meet him(her) on the path he(she) has chosen.
Help me to avoid bitterness and envy of those whose children have succeeded in ways I wanted mine to succeed.
Help me to let go of my dreams and love what is good in the dreams of my child.

Ronda De Sola Chervin

My child's marriage

Lord God I am so tempted sometimes to interfere in my children's marriages; also in the way they bring up their children.

I know I must not and I know it would damage my relationship with them, so please help me to keep my mouth shut and just be there for them, supporting them, and giving them advice only when they ask for it!

However I can pray for them and I do now – that you would protect them and be with them in all the difficult times of marriage and parenthood.

Keep them committed to you and to each other. Help them to, together, look to you for their strength, guidance, love, and all they need.

Sometimes I ache and fear for them, but I trust in you, O Lord; their times are in your hands.

Grandmother's Prayers

Bless my grandchildren

Thank you, God, for each of my dear little grandchildren that I may love without great burden, watch with delight, receive their tiny loving responses.

Help me to enjoy being a secondary character in the lives of my grandchildren, not first, but still very cherished.

Give my children wisdom to bring them up in a way that will open them to you.

Helen Ross

I miss my grandchild

Dear Jesus,
I'd give all the pictures on my refrigerator for just one hug from my grandson. It seems so long since the last time I held him. Six months is a long time in his four-year-old life. Take my empty heart, heavenly Father, and fill it up with the joy of child's laughter.

Anonymous

My Family's Spirituality

Choose for yourselves this day
whom you will serve ...
But as for me and my house,
we will serve the LORD.
Joshua 24:15

Enable them to be lights

Thank you, Jesus, for our children.
Heal in them any hidden memories and
unconscious fears
which they have received from us
through our inadequacies as parents.
May your Holy Spirit arm them against the
dangers and temptations of our society which
damage their health and ruin their relationships.
Protect them from evil influences, and enable
them to be lights of your truth and your love
among their friends and those who come into
contact with them. So through them may your
Father and their Father be glorified.

John Gunstone

Praying together

Come Holy Spirit, teach us how to pray together as a family, so that we may honour God, praise him and listen to his word. So that Jesus may sweeten our relationships, give us honesty in expressing our needs, and help us to forgive each other and support each other.

Anonymous

Wisdom how to pray

Father, please give me your wisdom to know how to pray for my children. I lift their specific needs to you now. I forgive (name) for hurting me and disappointing me; please help me to love them with your love and to walk in constant forgiveness.

Lord, show me appropriate Scriptures to pray for them. I release ...... into your hands, and ask you to work in their lives according to your plan and purpose. I commit them into your care and trust you to draw them to yourself by the power of the Holy Spirit. Thank you in Jesus' name for your work of grace in their lives. Amen.

Quin Sherrer

The following prayers are based on Scripture

Lord, teach our children how to cleanse their ways by taking heed and keeping watch on themselves according to your Word, conforming their lives to it. May they seek you with all their hearts, inquiring of you and yearning for you. Let them not wander or step aside (either in ignorance or wilfully) from your commandments.

Psalm 119:1–11

Thank you, Lord, that you know the plans you have for (name) plans to prosper and not to harm, plans to give ...... hope and a future. Thank you that when we call upon you and come and pray to you, you listen. When we seek you, we find you.

Jeremiah 29:11–13

I release these gifts you've given me, Lord, and place my children in your hands. I thank you that you love them more than I do, that your plans for them are plans of welfare and peace.

Jeremiah 29:11

Father, may my children fulfil your plan and purpose for their lives. May the Spirit of the Lord be upon them – the Spirit of wisdom and understanding, the Spirit of counsel and of power, the Spirit of knowledge and of the fear of the Lord.

Isaiah 11:2

May they walk in the fruit of the Spirit: love, joy, peace, patience, goodness, faithfulness, gentleness and self-control.

Galatians 5:22–23

May my child "live a life worthy of the Lord and please you in every way: bearing fruit in every good work, growing in the knowledge of God, being strengthened with all power according to your glorious might so that (name) may have great endurance and patience, and joyfully give thanks to the Father, who has qualified him(her) to share in the inheritance of the saints in the kingdom of light. For he has rescued him(her) from the dominion of darkness and brought him(her) into the kingdom of the Son he loves, in whom ...... has redemption, the forgiveness of sins."

Colossians 1:10–14

God, I ask you to fill (name) with the knowledge of your will through all spiritual wisdom and understanding in order that he(she) might live a life worthy of the Lord and may please you in every way, growing in the knowledge of God, being strengthened with all power, according to your glorious might so that he(she) may have great endurance and patience, and joyfully give thanks to the Father, who has qualified him(her)to share in the inheritance of the saints in the kingdom of light.

Colossians 1:9–12

To know compassion

I pray that my children will be evermore like Jesus. I pray that when they see needs in the world around them they will be moved with compassion. I also pray that they will know God's compassion in their own lives. Help me as a parent to be His heart and voice and arms of compassion to my children.

William and Nancie Carmichael

Set our hearts on fire

Set our hearts on fire with love to you, O Christ our God, that in its flame we may love You with all our heart, with all our mind, with all our soul, and with all our strength and our neighbours as ourselves, so that, keeping your commandments, we may glorify you, the giver of all good gifts.

Eastern Orthodox church

Give me discernment

Father God, creator of all things, I thank you for the gift of my children. ... I ask you to send Christian friends into their lives to help them and be a godly influence. Lord, what an awesome privilege and responsibility to be a parent. Help me discern when my children need my prayers or my help. Give me wisdom to be the parent I need to be, and help me to be an understanding friend to them.

Quin Sherrer

That they might accept Jesus

Lord, I'm grieved because my parents / children haven't accepted Jesus as Saviour. I know that it is not your will that any should perish. I stand in the gap in prayer for them, bringing them to your throne of grace and mercy. God, have mercy on them. May the Holy Spirit woo them to Jesus. God, grant them repentance that they may escape from the trap of the devil.

2 Peter 3:9; 2 Timothy 2:25

Being a Mother, Wife

and Much More

My soul finds rest in God alone;
my salvation comes from him.
He alone is my rock and my salvation;
he is my fortress, I shall never be shaken.
Psalm 62:1,2

Help

A prayer to be said
When the world has gotten you down,
and you feel rotten
and you're too doggone tired to pray,
and you're in a big hurry,
and besides, you're mad at
everybody. ... Help.

Charles Swindoll

I am powerless

Dear God, I am powerless and my life is unmanageable without your love and guidance. I come to you tonight because I believe that you can restore and renew me to meet my needs tomorrow and to help me meet the needs of my children.

Since I cannot manage my life or affairs, I have decided to give them to you. I put my life, my will, my thoughts, my desires and ambitions in your hands. I give you each of my children.

I give you all of me: the good and the bad, the character defects and shortcomings, my selfishness, resentments and problems.

I know that you will work them out in accordance with your plan.

Anonymous

Gratitude

Lord, I pray that my child will develop a grateful heart. Help me to demonstrate gratitude in my own life. Help us in this self-absorbed generation to give You joyful thanks.

William and Nancie Carmichael

Equipping them to resist

Oh, God, help me to equip my children to resist temptation.

We have taken our beautiful world and damaged it so badly for them. We have filled it with physical threat and moral dangers. All this propaganda for sexual licence, Lord; for breaking laws we don't like; all the drinking – and now these soul- and mind-scarring drugs.

Oh, dear God, arouse in me such a sense of what is truly right and truly wrong that I can convey it to them. Give me the words to express these things, and the courage to say them.

God, keep me close to my children, so that they aren't afraid to talk to me freely. And give me the patience to listen, no matter how inconvenient the times when they come.

God, give me the wisdom to guide them, and the wisdom to keep quiet when that is best. Don't let me invade their privacy. Don't let me live their lives for them. Don't let me betray their trust.

God, fortify me so that I can fortify my children. Give me the strength of character to demonstrate through my own behaviour what I claim to believe.

Oh, God, help me to equip my children to live decent happy lives in a world where it is so hard to be good.

Marjorie Holmes

Give me patience

Oh, God, give me patience! With this child who's telling his eager, long-winded story. Let me keep smiling and pretend I'm enthralled. If I don't, if I cut him off he'll not only be hurt, he may not come to me with something really important next time. But, dear Lord, help to guide him gently to the climax soon.

Oh, God, give me patience! With this baby who's dawdling over his food. He must eat, the doctor says, and I mustn't coax, threaten, or grab him and shake him as I'm tempted to – even though I know it would only make things worse and damage us both. Help me to sit quietly waiting, waiting, learning patience.

Oh, God, give me patience! With this boring old lady who wants me to look at all the pictures of her grandchildren and listen (again) to her oft-told tales. Help me to remember that I may be just as difficult some day, and that by showing warm interest I can add a little joy to her few remaining days instead of resenting the time she's taking. ...

Oh, God, give me patience – as I wait for a friend who is late, or for a line that's busy, or for traffic to clear. Let me be fully aware of my surroundings as I wait ... the scent and colour and sound of the very air. Help me to realize that no time is really wasted in this life so long as we are fully aware to the moment, so long as we are aware.

Oh, God, give me patience – with myself! With my follies, my hasty words, my own mistakes. The times when I seem a hopeless bumbler unworthy of friend or family or the company of any human being, so that I get into a panic and think, "Why am I taking up space on the earth? Why can't I just flee, vanish into eternity, simply disappear?" Help me to stop wrestling with remorse. Taking a futile inventory. Waking up in the night to berate myself for "things I ought to have done and things I ought not to have done". Reassure me, oh God, that there is health and hope and goodness in me, and that if I just have patience they will take over. I'll become the person I want to be and that you expect me to be.

Marjorie Holmes

Never too late

Lord, I love my children so much and yet sometimes I feel I've let them (and you) down so very badly. I look back and remember the harsh words I spoke out of impatience and anger, the misuse of my 'power' over them. The many times I hustled them out of the way to welcome others into our home – do they feel they were less important?

Lord, has this built in them an insecurity, a reserve with others? Have I damaged them for life?

Lord God their heavenly Father, please heal the hurts I have caused them, please build them up in your love. And Father as I have asked their forgiveness so I ask you to forgive me.

Thank you that you can heal and thank you that it is never too late – that I can build up my children in my love, in positive and affirming words and actions, in showing them that my past behaviour was a sign of my own immaturity and not a lack of love, that they have always been and always will be not just special and important to me, but a part of me.

Bring back the children

Lord, it seems sometimes that my arms aren't long enough or my lap isn't big enough. I wish I could stretch my arms out and out to embrace all my children. These here about the table now, and those who are away, off to their meetings or their dates or far away in their own homes.

I am suddenly aware of them, all of them wherever they are, and the excitement and wonder and pain of their lives are almost too much to comprehend.

I am so thrilled about them, so proud of them, and so worried about them too – all at once. I want suddenly to reach out and touch them, the warmth of their flesh, the feel of their hair, to draw them physically in.

I want to hold them on my lap again, the big ones and the little ones, all at once. I want to tuck them in their beds under the same familiar roof. I want to lock the door and go to sleep knowing they're all safe in the shelter of this house.

Lord, I wish I could have all my children back – now, this moment, at once. But since I can't, you who are everywhere, reach them for me, keep them safe in the shelter of my love.

Marjorie Holmes

My parenthood

Lord, you certainly give clear directives to parents. That I should lay up Your words "in my heart and in my soul", and that I should teach them to my children at all times (Deuteronomy 11:18,19).

What a sobering thought that our parenthood is part of our "works" that will go through the fire of Your judgment.

Keep this imperative in the forefront of my thinking, Father, for as I obey You, I know that You will be sovereign Lord over my children. How they need You in these times, Lord! How we, their parents, need You.

Catherine Marshall (adapted)

Stand by me

Oh, God, I was so cross with the children today. Forgive me. Oh, God, I was so discouraged, so tired, and so unreasonable. I took it out on them. Forgive me. Forgive me my bad temper, my impatience, and most of all my yelling. I cringe to think of it. My heart aches. I want to go down on my knees beside each little bed and wake them up and beg them to forgive me. Only I can't, it would only upset them more. I've got to go on living with the memory of this day. My unjust tirades. The guilty fear in their eyes as they flew about trying to appease me. Thinking it was all their fault – my troubles, my disappointments.

Dear God, the utter helplessness of children. Their vulnerability before this awful thing, adult power. And how forgiving they are, hugging me so fervently at bedtime, kissing me good night. And all I can do now is to straighten a cover, move a toy fallen out of an upthrust hand, touch a small head burrowed into a pillow, and beg in my heart, "Forgive me."

Lord, in failing these little ones whom you've put into my keeping, I'm failing you. Please let your infinite patience and goodness fill me tomorrow. Stand by me, keep your hand on my shoulder. Don't let me be so cross with my children.

Marjorie Holmes

It's all too much

Lord, it's all so busy. My parents need me, my children need me, my husband should have much more of my time and attention, I'm so concious of that. My work takes up so much time, the house gets neglected and then I feel guilty and burdened by it all. Father, as I come to you now help me to be quiet for a moment and not do all the talking. Show me what you consider important as opposed to urgent, show me your priorities. Help me to be conscious of you beside me, that I might be wise in all I do and know your peace. I would open myself to you now and ask you to bring order into what seems like chaos in me. Thank you Lord.

Lord, don't forget me

Lord, you know how busy I must be today. If I forget you, please don't forget me.

General Lord Jacob Astley (1579–1652)
– before the Battle of Edgehill

My parents are getting old

Lord, it hurts so much to see my parents grow feeble and suffer with infirmities. Heavenly Father, I commit them into your loving care. Only you know the number of their days. I thank you that because they know Jesus, they are assured of eternal life with him – where there'll be no aching, deformed bodies or minds affected by disease.

Give me the patience, kindness, and gentleness I need to respond in love to the many demands made on me in caring for them. I thank you for them, Lord. You knew exactly the parents I needed. I now release them from my expectations! Touch their bodies with your healing power. Keep them from feeling lonely, unwanted, and useless. I praise you for my parents, Lord, and what they have meant to me. Now in their latter years, may I be to them what they need. I come asking this in the name of your blessed Son, Jesus. Amen.

Quin Sherrer

Worth more than rubies

Lord, may my husband be won to you without words – simply by my behaviour – as he sees the purity and reverence of my life. God, may it be so! Lord, may my husband treat me with respect, loving me as Christ loved the church. As a wife, may I be of more worth than rubies to my husband, bringing him good and not harm all the days of our lives. Thank you for this man you've given me for a life partner. Show me ways to express to him how much I revere and trust him. Help me to learn to pray more effectively for him. Amen.

Quin Sherrer

May I be a good wife

Lord, I desire to be the helper for my husband that you want me to be and that he needs. May I do him good all the days of his life and may he have full confidence in me. I want to watch over the affairs of our household wisely. Lord, help us to mutually love and respect one another. May our home be a place of peace and security where you are honoured and worshipped. I ask in Jesus' name. Amen.

Quin Sherrer

The tender trap

O Lord, I'm so tired and lonely and blue I'm a little afraid. I'm so sick of house-work, sick of the children. They get on my nerves so I could scream (and do). I'm even sick of my husband at the moment – I wish he'd go away on a business trip. Or I wish I could get away for a change. ... I want to be somebody else for a while. Maybe the girl I used to be, or maybe a woman I haven't even met yet. A beautiful poised woman with a mind and life of her own. Only I can't. There's never any going back to what you used to be. And for the moment there's no going ahead. There's only the present which sometimes seems such a trap. ...

Maybe my husband feels trapped too, going day after day to the same job. ... And the women who leave their houses to fight traffic or crowd-ed buses to get to work every day. Maybe they're screaming too somewhere inside.

Lord, help me to realise how lucky I am here. Turn my fantasies of escape to some purpose. Bless that person you surely meant me to be, instead of this self-pitying drudge. Recreate me in her image. Help me to see that she is not some superior creature that would evolve out of other circumstances, but that she lives inside me.

Marjorie Holmes

The woman I was meant to be

Lord, I now affirm and claim [the woman inside you meant me to be]. I claim her poise, her calm, her patience, her cheerfulness, her self-control. I claim her beauty. I claim her renewed mind.

I claim her for my children.
   She will be a better mother.
I claim her for my husband.
   She will be a better wife.

Marjorie Holmes (adapted)

By my example

Lord, help me to know how to encourage my children to be kind, patient, generous, pure-minded and self-controlled. Father help me to be able to teach these by example, to develop these same virtues in my own life.

Other Prayers

God is our refuge and strength,
an ever-present help in trouble.
Therefore we will not fear,
though the earth give way
and the mountains fall into the heart of the sea,
though its waters roar and foam
and the mountains quake with their surging.
Psalm 46:1–4

Illness in the family

O God, our Father, bless and help (name). Give him(her) courage and patience, endurance and cheerfulness to bear all weakness and all pain; and a mind at rest, which will make the recovery all the quicker. Give to all doctors, surgeons and nurses who attend him(her) skill in their hands, wisdom in their minds, and gentleness and sympathy in their hearts. Lord Jesus, show us that your healing touch has never lost its ancient power. This we ask for thy love's sake. Amen.

William Barclay (adapted)

Safety for travel

God our Father, be with us as we travel. Be our safety every mile of the way. Make us attentive, cautious and concerned about our fellow travellers. Make our highways safe and keep us from all danger. Guide us to our destination for today and may it bring us one day closer to our final destination with you. We pray this in Jesus' name. Amen

Sacred Heart Auto League

Holidays

Father, thank you that we can go away together on holiday. Away from the pressures of our daily lives here at home. Thank you that we can spend time resting, playing, seeing new places, meeting new people. Bless our time, Lord, please, refresh us in body and in mind, ready to return home restored and the better for our holiday. Protect us in our travelling, and those we leave behind.

Be my child's vision

Be Thou [my child's] vision. O Lord of my heart,
Be all else but naught to him, save that Thou art; ...

Be Thou his wisdom, be Thou his true word,
Be Thou ever with him, and he with Thee, Lord;
Be Thou his great Father, and he Thy true son;
Be Thou in him dwelling, and he with Thee one.

Be Thou his breastplate, his sword for the fight;
Be Thou his whole armour, be Thou his true might;
Be Thou his soul's shelter, be Thou his strong tower;
O raise Thou him heavenward, great Power of my power.

May he not seek riches nor man's empty praise;
Be Thou his inheritance now and always;
Be Thou and Thou only the first in his heart:
O Sovereign of heaven, I pray his treasure Thou art.

Ancient Irish hymn
Tr. Mary Elizabeth Byrne & Eleanor Henrietta Hull
(adapted)

Working mother

Jesus, it was not my plan to work when my baby was so small. Yet, when I prayed for a way to stay home no way seemed possible.

So, as I reluctantly leave my darling with a child minder, ... may [my] baby not feel abandoned. Let me be thankful to you, God, for providing another woman with a desire to nuture little babies. May the guardian angels of the babies in her home surround and protect them. Amen.

Anonymous

Refuge for my children

I pray that my children will be kept safe, safe from physical harm and especially safe from the evil one, who would destroy. I pray that my children will have that wonderful sense of being cradled by God, even in the stormy times of their lives, that they will run to the shelter of the Lord's presence for refuge.

William and Nancie Carmichael

Single mother

O my Jesus, I feel so lonely, frightened and bewildered. I never thought I would be raising my children alone. I cannot pretend to be happy in the midst of this tragedy but I need special grace not to allow any bitterness to poison my children's lives.

Give me a spirit of forgiving love and patient hope and may I receive your spousal love for me in such abundance that I may be able to overflow with this love to my children. May they love their father in spite of everything and may they find in the Fatherhood of God a recompense for whatever is lacking in their own father. Please give us ways to meet our financial needs. Send my husband a spirit of justice to want to sustain the part of the support my children need in a steady, committed way.

Provide us, we ask you, with the love of our extended family and with many good Christian friends. Bless us all, dear Jesus, now and forever, Amen.

Ronda De Sola Chervin

Our home

In your great mercy, O Lord, grant that this may be a good day in this home. Save us from becoming casual with each other. Save us from lack of self-discipline. Save us from any discourtesy. Bless any who shall come over our doorstep, any who shall sit at our table, or share talk with us over the phone.

Let us use our home and the treasured things we have gathered about us to give others joy. Make us each discreet in our conversation, and loving and loyal to each other. And to you we should give all the glory and praise. Amen.

Rita Snowden

Contentment

I pray that my children will learn godliness with contentment, and that in doing so, they will become satisfied with what God gives them.

William and Nancie Carmichael

I offer my life

Lord, I offer my daily life with my children, as a prayer for all the children of the world, especially those who are unloved, mal-treated, sexually abused, starving, lonely, bul-lied, orphaned, or afraid.

Lord, I offer my struggle with the demands of parenthood as a prayer for other parents, those who face similar difficulties, and those whose problems are different.

Lord, I offer my delight in my children as a prayer for childless couples, bereaved parents, single parents who ache for someone to share the load, adopted children who have been told the truth too late, women who have had abortions, aborted babies, and for all the secure and con-tented children too.

Angela Ashwin

Sources of Prayers

Ashwin, Angela, *Patterns not Padlocks* (Guildford: Eagle, 1992).

Askew, Eddie, *Disguises of Love* (Leprosy Mission).

Astley, Jacob, from *The Oxford Book of Prayer*, ed. George Appleton (Oxford: OUP, 1985).

Barclay, William, *A Book of Everyday Prayer* (NewYork: Harper & Brothers, 1959).

Brandt, Leslie and Edith, as quoted in *Draw Me* (Ann Arbor Michigan: Servant Publications, 1990).

Carmichael, William and Nancie, *God Bless My Child* (Wheaton, Illinois: Tyndale House Publishers, 1995).

Chervin, Ronda De Sola, *A Mother's Treasury of Prayers,* op. cit.

De Sola, Diana, *A Mother's Treasury of Prayers,* op. cit.

Graham, Ruth Bell, quoted in *The Gift of a Child* (Oxford: Lion Publishing, 1982).

Gunstone, John, *Prayers for Healing* (Godalming: Highland, 1987).

Holmes, Marjorie, *I've Got to Talk to Somebody, Lord* (London: Hodder & Stoughton, 1969).

Huggett, Joyce, *Conflict: Friend or Foe?* (Eastbourne: Kingsway).

Marshall, Catherine & Leonard Le Sourd, *My Personal Prayer Diary* (London, Hodder & Stoughton,1988).

Mattison, Judith, adapted from, *Delight in the Gift,*

Mother Theresa in *Prayers* (Nashville, Thomas Nelson, 1993).

Schaffer, Ulrich, quoted in *The Gift of a Child,* op. cit.

Sherrer, Quin and Garlock, Ruthanne, *How to Pray for Your Family and Friends* (Eastbourne: Kingsway, 1990), *The Spiritual Warrior's Prayer Guide* (Guildford: Eagle, 1992) and *A Woman's Guide to Spiritual Warfare* (Guildford: Eagle, 1991).

Snowden, Rita, *Woman's Book of Prayers* (London: Fount, 1985).

Stroud, Marion, *The Gift of a Child* (Oxford: Lion, 1982) and *The Gift of Friends* (Oxford: Lion, 1983).

Swindoll, Charles, p 18: *Growing Strong in the Season of Life* (Grand Rapids: Zondervan, 1994);

p 58: *Prayers* (Nashville:Thomas Nelson, 1993).